A Storm by Any Other Name

PC Scheponik

PS Books
Philadelphia, Pennsylvania

A Storm by Any Other Name
by PC Scheponik

A Storm by Any Other Name Copyright 2011
Published by PS Books, a division of Philadelphia Stories, Inc.

ISBN 13: 978-1-257-05882-2

Cover Image: "Solitary Splendor" by Lee Muslin, © 2011, used with permission. www.LeeMuslin.com

PS Books
93 Old York Road
Ste. 1/#1-753
Jenkintown, PA 19046
www.psbookspublishing.org

A Storm by Any Other Name

To Shirley,

You are, have been, and always will be the best part of the journey.

With all my love,

Pete

Contents

Songs of Self

Old Vamp at a Young Party

I watch them move across the floor, one with the beat,
music pumping, indiscreet,
Their bodies humping in rhythmic waves.
They are in the moment, ecstatic, wanton,
borderline depraved.
How they make me hungry.
How they save me from myself, from age
that has taken over my life in every way.
I look with longing, almost say what is on my mind:
I'd like to suck the youth right out of them,
till I could bump and grind again.
Sorry old vampire—the envious kind,
voyeur of beauty, with oh-so-hungry eyes;
their frenzy stakes me.
I squirm in my seat, try to defeat
the coming of day, the knowledge that I
am too old to play, that the mirror is my enemy,
While they go on writhing to the melody,
youth and desire, thriving and free.
I slip out the back door, sullen to be me,
away from the dance, afraid of the fire,
aware of the fact that passion and romance
have long ago expired.
The coffin awaits without pose or prance,
offering me my only remaining chance,
lid tight on the darkness of my dreams.

Ghost Writer

Let infamy make no ghost of me,
leave me locked in this world after death,
to roam the shelves of library stacks,
to wander the endless links of the Net,
to walk through words,
those walls of hearts and minds,
trying to connect, to make it this time,
sucked back to life with a single breath,
airy resurrection, spoken into being,
with consonant vowel perfection,
What will I say?
What will I be?
What will I mean?
to them,
to me,
once time and eternity
each take a hand
and stretch me ever after.

The Lessons

It is morning, the sun still rubbing
last night's clouds from her eyes,
and he sees himself in the mirror,
pushing sixty, but hair still dark
with mousse and water, eyes still
Atlantic blue on an August afternoon,
chest and pecs still laced with curls,
that manhood he yearned for,
long after the first erection,
the first time he came,
hot white gushes of self and love
that cooled like cream all over his fingers,
glued him to maleness, his destiny,
his love, his portion of this life,
his tribe, the muscled comers
battling dragons of desire,
the need to be good,
to be trained by a woman,
caged in the fleshy vault of her body,
tamed by her love.

After Hours

The club is deserted during the day,
just the empty chairs,
the glass walls that display
the sea that rears its diamond-studded blue,
wave after wave, as if to prove
something like beauty, something like truth,
perhaps divinity in order to soothe
the wayfarer's soul that yearns horizonward
in a story as old as time.
Sitting among the empty chairs,
I am riding the song in my mind,
the sea and sky coming to me
in metered beats of the sublime,
the flood of these words—
so open, so infinite, so free,
I don't know where they begin or I end,
this ability to be an undulation in eternity,
this raw power I have learned to ride,
this rising tide of ecstasy.

Butterflies

I admire them, those who have befriended age,
thinning hair and sagging skin neither a challenge
nor a source of rage,
those who move through their days,
butterflies among the flowers.
With tissue-winged wobblings,
they pass the hours,
dancing at the edges of life,
sipping nectar memories, living quite
vicariously through the garden goings on
around them.
I am both forlorn and happy
I have found them,
An onlooker with glass box and pins,
awaiting his turn for legs and arms to thin
like hair,
to be without hope, without promise,
without care,
dancing so lightly, as if on air,
buttering these last moments
I fly.

Smokers

I enjoy going there, to the back of the ship,
like a place of punishment where they send
all the bad ones—rule breakers and edge dwellers
who seem to relish the catwalk, the tightrope,
the ancient jungle bridge, long abandoned
that threatens to break with every step,
send its crossers headlong into the depths
of rocky hell below.
I enjoy being with the bad boys, the naughty girls,
breathing and blowing the smoke they blow,
doing and knowing the things they know,
their red edges glowing like miniature Mars warrior gods—
all of them fighting the metal rod laws that would corset us all
till we can hardly move, stallions in stalls who barely breathe.
But not the wild ones, not these, they are undeceived
as if they have some secret knowledge that gives permission,
lets them do as they please,
drawing in air, letting out the white genie curls
born of their mouths, fire breathers—all .
I smell the smoldering chaos they hold in their hearts.
I can feel their call, and I come, like one
who has held it in too long,
wave after wave of me, as if my soul
could spurt and run in wild waste abandon,
like these whose lungs go up in smoke,
the warm curls of their essence, rising
like incense in obeisance to their own wills,
these who blithely spill themselves in hot oblations,
Caesars of the kingdom they have made to come.

Game of Life

My youth is long gone.
I know that now,
and groan in grief for its going.
This pain too deep for the knowing.
This life, no good for the growing, anymore,
the soil barren, the sky, without tears.
There's a dustbowl for the blowing
and a promise of years without seed,
without sowing, but not without owing
the heart, the soul, to the company store
that stole two crowns:
one from the governor,
one from God.
And the shovel will not enter the earth, too dry,
too hard to let me dig my way back in.
And the memory of the garden with its fruit
and knowledge grows dim.
We don't get to choose our exits and our entrances
any more than our sins.
The odds are stacked against us in a game we cannot win.

Knock and It Shall Be…

We take our troubles, each of us,
swaddle them in blankets warm as hearts that beat,
cuddling our infant miseries, who wawl and shriek,
the need to eat as strong in them as, in us, the need to feed.
We bare the breast, slip the drizzled nipple between
the puckered lips and let them suck the life from us,
drip by succulent drip,
until we almost come apart from the sorrowed joy of it,
from the girl and boy of it, from the game and toy of it all.
And when we run aground, bone dry, we call out to the stars
In a stark, resounding shout:
"More! More! More!"
Till dry-breasted and exhausted, we kneel against the door,
Knocking, knocking, knocking,
waiting in disbelief that it will be opened.

The Remnant

When I close my eyes,
sometimes, I feel young again,
firm of flesh, firmer of purpose,
willing to bend the rules
to make my mark,
press myself into this fabric of being,
the way the hand sinks into the sand,
momentary shape
before the waves come,
erase the proof that we
can scoop a way for ourselves,
make an effigy of dreams
in the granular scheme of matter,
temporal genes that scatter
like grains in sudden wind,
disappearing in the corona's rim,
so bright with burning.
Our right to yearning is divine
as our will to survive,
leave some remnant of ourselves
behind,
some artifact carved in stone.

No Reason

No reason to be bitter
because the chest has sagged,
the balls have been tugged down,
by gravity's heavy hand.
No need to resent
the cock, now bent
goes soft and sour.
You had your hour,
strutting codpiece upon the stage.
The fickle pickle oft assuaged
by hand or mouth or sweet peach cunt.
Oh how the juices made
your milk and honey run.
So that, now, at the time
that the clock strikes done,
there is no cause for anger
because the one
will no longer do for her,
or him, or you,
and the message is loud and clear:
You are through!
You are through!
There's no reason to resist,
no reason to make a list
of what ifs,
no reason to spurn adieu.
There's just no reason.

The Vision

Who was it that I saw
when I glanced in the window,
as I passed by?
So stern-faced, pursed lips,
furrowed brow above his eyes—
almost angry at the world,
ready to hurl an expletive or two
at the first person who dared
breathe air or cross his path.
Here was a fool-hearted dozer
in need of a laugh,
a sharp-eyed poser who didn't have
a clue, how lost, how driven he was
with every thought he had,
every step he took,
every breath he drew.
Here was a portrait of modern man,
Cubist style, face askew,
self-image twisted in ways
he never knew possible,
a living Picasso of his own making,
real-live art, a self-portrait taken
and framed in glass.
Oh the electrons, protons, and photons
holding fast to the see-through soul
of the store's window on whom such
vision fell.
At first, I thought of Dorian Gray, then
of Dante's journey through Hell.
But what does it matter, the reason
or the way the damage is done.
I can tell you that there's no undoing.
So for all the prowess, all the pain,

all the pursuing,
what was ever really gained
but the ruing of it all.
Tomorrow forecasts only more of the same,
and the only relief is the clouds that shade
and the rain that falls,
washing the vision away.

When I Am Old

When I am too old to mount love's pleasured hips,
let me give service to its splendors through my lips.

When I am too old to eat and drink,
let me be nourished and quenched with the thought I think.

When I am too old to walk by the sea,
let me sit in the sun on the balcony and set my gull's heart
    completely free.

When I am too old to speak my mind,
let me rest in the care of hearts and hands that are kind.

When I am too old to draw my last breath,
let me softly exhale and run free with death.

II

Let death be a field of endless flowers,
with nothing to fear and no need for hours,
with only beginnings and no more ends,
with only people who are true friends,
with no sense of loss and no touch of pain,
with no need to win, nothing more to gain,
a perfect estate where happiness reigns.

The Lover

My life's wake glistens in moonlit memory,
the waters christened with the years behind me,
a wide, glowing stretch that slowly shrinks
to a single silver thread, bright instinct
to hold on to all.
My heart grows full as I recall
the life that I have had, that has had me,
a sterling temporality that seems almost like infinity
when viewed upon these dark waters,
Looking backwards from the stern,
I wrap both hands around the rail,
fleshy palms and fingers squeeze
as if, perchance, to prevail over metallic cold,
the warmth, the wonder of growing old,
still in love with this world.

The Vamp in Me

I've lived so long with the pain.
I don't know how to do without it.
To remove the stake from my night heart—
unthinkable.
How would I rise each night, so hungry,
the need to feed, burning in my veins.
A slave of shadows, I roam the grey hills of regret,
haunt the hollows of loss, the hunger for sun
always burning,
the need for light, as deep as the yearning
the night breeds in me,
bleeds in me dreams of a dark sea
stirring, stirring my emptiness
till my shrieks rise like cream and I fly unseen,
into the ravenous night.

The Undiscovered

Definitely a must do, discovery of a self
that lies buried beneath sandy consciousness
curled like a crab, legs tucked in tightly,
like a little wet stone,
waiting for the diggers to come,
shovels gulping to the ocean's background drone.
There is no coping with discovery.
Mirrors are everywhere and in every way
only too willing to put on display who we are.
Though there is always the option to close our eyes,
or like Oedipus, once we realize,
take the sharp-edged broach and dig,
groping through the sands with sharp-tongued spades
and Tiresian hands until we feel the wriggling of the one
who didn't get away, and lift it up, pry open its legs
to the light of day, let the sun in, where it rarely shines,
look deeply into the black mica pupils of the wriggler's wild eyes
and see, for the very first time, the undiscovered self.

We All Fly Solo

It's a sad and solitary game we play,
searching for answers,
living, loving along the way,
dying upon the chances we take,
the lives we touch, the hearts we break,
our own, as well as others.
There is no magic cure for this ill.
No spell or incantation will
free us from this quest.
Searching seems to be the state
when we are at our best.
And always with us, at our side,
our guide, named loneliness.

The Missing Piece

I can't find that piece of my heart I put away for safekeeping.
I thought I saw it in the red silk cup of a tulip, shimmering in the sun.
I thought I heard it in the trill of a goldfinch flying by.
I thought I felt it in an April breeze, gently stirring the magnolia trees.
I thought I smelled it in the sweet perfume of an Easter lily's tender bloom.
I thought I tasted it in the drops of rain upon my tongue.
I thought I recognized it in the innocent smile upon the face of a little child.
I felt I held it in my hand in a puppy's tail, wagging and wild.
I thought I caught a glimpse of it in the startled blue jay's sudden flight.
I was sure I had discovered it in the diamond dance of dust in light.
Then I woke and realized that life is a dream in which I try but
never find that missing piece.

American High

There are moments when I recall
the terror of the study hall
where no good came from idle minds
or monitors who wasted time
reading sports news or gaining points
with all the thugs by talking game,
or size, or joints, always the same old routine,
promise of prom with its football King and cheerleader Queen.
There was after all nothing in between
this bookend culture of American school,
where you never dared draw out of the lines
where there were quotas and yardsticks for being cool.
And principals and counselors didn't have time,
and teachers didn't want to hear it on their dime,
where being different was a major crime,
and the death sentence was spelled FAGGOT.

Getting to the Essence

There are times I like to strip myself down
to the bare essentials,
the way, as a young boy, I used to strip branches:
First the leaves with one clean pull,
then the green skin covering till
only the wet, white bark remained,
smooth as polished ivory inside,
buried like a soul, the cellulose marrow of bark bone,
tabernacled within the chlorophyll vein
where the liquid God of wonder, God of light reigned.
When I strip, I start with my family,
my job, my name, my sex,
it's quite a game, the undoing of me,
religion and memories next,
all the way back to the leaves, to the apple,
to the serpent, to the tree, to the promise of being divine,
down to the cellular structure of earth,
down to the dance of synaptic bursts,
those magical moments that seem to shine.

Songs of Faith

Somewhere

I often wonder if these words
are really messages in bottles,
one after the other,
hurled to the arms of waiting waves
who wash them away toward destiny.
Will I be rescued?
Will I be saved?
Or must I stay forever on this island,
scribbling my soul into letters
that become words, that have meanings,
which float upon the waters,
their kelpy fingers green with yearning
to take root in those children who eat the sun's fire,
drink the sea's tears,
these remnants of me adrift like prayers,
or cares, or the need to be connected
some way, somehow, somewhere.

The Reluctant

They always ask me why I am not in the books
on the shelves, being bought and sold,
broken like bread or given whole
to the hungry crowds
with their empty hearts and their open mouths,
nestlings or infants crying aloud to be suckled, to be fed.
Oh mother's milk! Oh crust of bread!
to save them from being dead inside.
They ask me why I choose to hide my light beneath a basket,
and I sigh,
when I think of the tisket,
when I think of the tasket
that comes with the feeding,
the regurgitation and sometimes the bleeding.
If I could create the perfect food,
the type that would satisfy the entire brood,
I might take delight in ministering to mouths.
But for now,
I'll simply continue to bake and leave it to others to take
and to break and to feed the gathering crowds.

A Story of Lines

I refuse to become just another line,
in a history of bitter lines,
just another life contained
between points argued and points made.
I will, if anything, become a ray,
go in a different direction,
branch out in holy ascension
toward a heaven of my own making.
From the beauty of moments,
I will fashion Daedalean wings.
From the truths of this world,
I will extract the notes to sing my songs,
high above the heads of those walkers of the line
who long to fly, who long to sing
but cannot find a way because of their need to cling
to the points of the well-apportioned line they know,
the line they keep, whether it breaks their hearts,
or burns their feet.
They must walk one way only, in order to meet the primordial
    need:
To know, first, where they are going, and only, then, to proceed.

The Reasons

These days he is coming back to himself,
the way one returns to a childhood home or a former school,
    looking for answers.
Things are different, although the same; the stone seems greyer,
    as if with age.
Everything is attic dust and library stacks that smell of old boxes
    and book mites.
He can tell, once again, for a moment, where he's going from
    where he's been—
the aches in certain joints, the love, the loss of family, of friends,
the bits and pieces of self auctioned off for quarters on the
    dollar, all of it, must go in the end.
But those parts he holds onto—an old medal, a faded photo,
a yellowed note whose ink has dried from navy blue to terra
    cotta brown,
the color of broken flower pots and abandoned sounds: moth
    wings beating,
crickets bleating like little lost anthracite lambs.
And he is the good shepherd of his own life; he holds the pieces
    in his own hands
that bleed like Christs's, from all the twisting, the turning, the
    trying to understand
the meaning, despite the distractions of the darkness, of the
    light, of the ever–passing
seasons and their endless demands.
These days, he's coming back to himself, and though the
    answers are not quite what he
expected, the reasons, oh the reasons are still the same.

As Such

As such, he viewed life, this earth, with its indigo skies and
diamond stars,
this world, with its emerald forests and white ice peaks,
this planet, with its coral beaches and turquoise seas
as a Mother, both beautiful and cruel who weened him
with mixed messages of intimate pleasures, of infinite pains,
till he couldn't measure beauty, treasure truth in any way
that would allow him to gain his independence,
sustain his freedom outside the flesh domain
of her Mother goddess folds—a prisoner of her womb,
with its red velvet walls and salt water seas,
and he, a hermit crab scuttling through the sharp glass grains,
cutting himself to fit her mold, to be, not to be,
as such, remains the question.

A Musing

Listening to the words of salvation, I find
so many instances of condemnation that I
unjoin my palms and throw them up
in a prayer of despair.
Such trickery of words and more,
of meanings—interpretations for the gleaning,
all of us bent over in the fields,
looking for grains and grapes
that will yield a thousand fold,
that will feed and bleed us into happiness,
into being whole,
that will heal the forever wound.
If we follow the Way, get the message straight
from the prophet's mouth—sacred words
from a hot ember voice, a roasted flesh tongue,
if we can decipher the holy one in the endless crowd.
How to uncircumcise the mind once it has been cut
by faith's sharp blade!
Where to seek, how to find the self in a heart
that has been filleted for the love of God!
I am so tired and empty from these divine charades
we have played from the very first day we decided
to dress and to walk out of the garden's gate.

Creation Up for Love

The sign on the bumper read:
"LOVE THE CREATOR
    NOT THE CREATION."
What does that mean,
when creation holds us
in maternal arms,
fills us with mystery
of what it is to taste,
to touch, to smell,
to hear, to see and be seen,
each of us, in ways unique,
suckled richly throughout our days
by the infinite energy of divine waves
in a cosmic sea, warm as sun love,
deep as eternity.
Should we ask creation how much she loves,
she would open her infinite arms
like the wings of an ascending dove,
sheltering us from harm, like the mother at the nest,
she would cover us in the safety of her feathered breast.
What does it mean to not love creation—
to deny ourselves all oblation
to the divinity within, without,
to reject who we are, were meant to be,
what our essence, our destiny is all about.
When we encounter creation, it should be
on bended knee as we shout to the stars our love.

Monologue

So many times I have wanted to say to you,
"It's not your fault."
How could you have known at six
what to do.
In front of Jesus with the bleeding heart,
His nail-pierced hands, promising Him you
would jump if He didn't part the waters
of the hospital stay, make a dry path home,
to that promised land of mother love.
And now, all these years later, still on your own,
pain packed up in bags, one by each side,
and the best that you can do is admit that you tried;
you really tried.

Need to Believe

Lately, I have taken a shining to atheism,
A way of thinking outside of the Godbox.
Bibbety, bobbety, boo,
no heaven, no hell,
no absolute rule will do,
a sea of freedom to sail through,
no bridges to be built,
just navigating the troubled waters,
a matter of perspective,
relative as time and space,
but it is the matter that calls to me,
cries out in vengeance for some sacred sake,
from Auschwitz, from Belsen, from Dachau,
with a thirst I cannot slake.
I can feel the heat of the ovens,
see the smoke choking out the sky.
I can smell the stench of the roasting flesh,
hear the zyklon throats that cry,
"Oh constellation of six-million yellow stars
burns a galactic stain, deep into the synaptic layers
of cosmologic membranes,
light from light, and nothing can restrain
the cries that rain, the tears that flame."
I can hear; I can hear them,
calling in the name of
in the name of
in the name of
needing to believe.

A Certain Story

One marriage ends; another begins
sons and daughters, sons and sons,
daughters and daughters,
a place for everyone.
The sins of the father, the mother denied,
put away with Gaia, locked deep inside
Pele's heart, burning, burning,
yearning, always yearning to start
again.
The garden, the garden,
the center of the garden;
it's always the same place,
I tell you, my friend,
"I hear there are two trees:
one for knowledge of everything,
one for never-ending life,
and for the story to begin
and for the story to end,
all it takes is just one bite."

Resurrection and Light

When I think of the dead,
those I loved and lost,
I can see them with my eyes opened wide,
not in front of me, like my hand or the sky,
or the hills and trees,
not like the visionaries,
the way the three children saw the Virgin at the cove,
but somewhere in the back of my mind I see
their faces—my father's, my grandparents', my
aunts' and uncles', my friends' who have passed away.
I can make them smile, enjoy their expressioned displays
as if they were alive.
I don't understand how this happens;
maybe there's an eye on the back of my eyes
so that when the pupil throws open its shutter
to let in the sun's light, some inward pupil
does the same.
But I tell you, I can see them, can even name
the number of their wrinkles, the layers of their hair,
the individual shades of their eyes.
This video screen inside my head can synthesize
the past with present, resurrect the dead
with the light that glows in my mind,
And the two become one.
And the mourner's tears are dried.
And death is no more.

Garden Story

A person, a person, God must be a person.
The anthropomorphic cries out for this.
Only in the image and likeness of the human
can we fall to our knees and plead
the narcissistic in us that bleeds
beating hearts to hungry suns
or paschal lambs to warrior thrones.
Divinity demands a ransom.
The infinity within us reaches out
with stigmatic hands.
And voices loud with martyrdom shout
Amen! Amen! Amen!
There is no end to this inner need,
to this covenant of make and believe,
of sacrifice to intercede,
of raising flowers and burning weeds,
in the name of this garden of gods.

The Joyful

I have walked away from the wood pile,
away from the blade that threatened to open
the rich jugular in my throat, let the velvet blood flow,
for the kingdom, the power, and the gory glory of God,
a naked child inside the body of an old man.
I danced down the hillside, David without ark or covenant.
I am through with cutting of every kind.
Let the Samson in me grow back his eyes and locks.
Let him take the jawbone of an ass and play joyful songs.
I have found the offering for which I have longed:
the beauty of the garden, where it has always been,
rising like a tree of life, full bloom, in the center of my heart.

Humilitatus

I've lived so long at the foot of the altar;
I don't know how to live without the need to believe
that somewhere in this universe
of black holes and white dwarves,
of worms and antimatter, that
there is someone behind the curtain
dispensing brains and hearts, courage and a way home;
that the witches and their flying monkeys
will be controlled,
will be controlled.
I've lived so long with incense;
I've grown accustomed to the smell
and to the hope that its white smoke
will be pontiff to heaven and not to hell.
I cannot do without the ritual of the pain
the bleeding of the lamb of God,
a Eucharistic game I must play,
though the stain of guilt remains and remains.
I've learned to make a magic of the grapes and of the grains,
a solitary hunger when sated refrains and refrains.
I've learned to make confession for sins I do again and again,
but there is no easy answer, no practice that can contain this
 need in me,
this need to be prostrate at the feet that forever bleed,
like the hands and the heart and the face that seeds eternity
with curses and grace.
Oh confusion of the Word, the words, the words
we take and break like bread and backs and hearts
to make our own—all of us at our self-made altars of
human need, and dust of stars, and hearts of stone,
bowed in the name of eternity, built upon promises within and
 afar,
worshipping what we cannot know, can never know.

Songs of Family

The Touching Way

We talk about our family, my sister and I,
gluing together the slivers and shards
with excuses and forgiveness,
varnishing the past with understanding—
layer upon layer until our lacquered history
holds together and shines—
something we can look upon, find our reflections,
buff them with soft-cloth memories
until they are bright as tears.
We are very careful, take greatest care,
not to press too hard, life and love are fragile,
and this choice to reconcile, whispers like the voice
of God.
We listen and hear, take every chance there is
to repair a fresh start, attentive to every nuance.
Beginning again is a delicate art that takes time
and effort on everyone's part.
Reaching with Michelangelo fingers,
we touch our way back to love.

Tough Love

My wife tells me she wants a divorce from our children,
and I am inclined to agree:
the drugs, the bickering, the financial instabilities,
the oldest one's recent separation, brought on by
his wife's infidelities,
and the two grandsons dumped in the rapids,
happy home canoe flipped upside down.
We can see them swirling in separation's currents,
their swimming skills undeveloped,
the fear, real, that they might drown.
And we, still standing on solid ground,
toss out our life-saving love,
hoping to reach them in time,
praying that they'll bob back above,
be able to grab the line,
to be drawn back to safety,
to the sure banks of love.

The Weening

He tells me his mommy goes a lot of places,
and he doesn't get to spend much time with her,
his seven years, as yet, unable to figure out anything
but loss of time,
The loss of love, of marriage, of father and mother together
holding high above him the roof of happy home,
not yet real.
This young one so alone with the thoughts of his own,
unsure how to feel, tells me he doesn't want to talk
about the divorce, and I acquiesce, unable to guess
what it is like at seven, the age of reason and
first Holy Communion, to discover there are times
love does not last, that sorrow must have its season,
that the star wished upon does not respond,
the wish a creature made of heart and air,
tumbling through eternity,
like a broken dream or an unanswered prayer.

The Inside

On our way back from the beach to the condo,
the youngest one tells me,
"Grandpa, I have two shells,
a big one and a little one—
one for Ethan and one for me.
"See," he demonstrates, "how
the small one fits inside the big one."
And I think of their two lives,
the way they have always been,
the older taking care of the younger.
And I wonder how their lives will be
after the divorce,
the small one taking shelter in the big one,
both taking shelter in their grandparents'
love.
And I am so happy to have built this house
upon rock,
a fortress that will stand strong in the storm—
a safe place among the shifting sands.

Second Chance

It was early in the morning when the smooth,
grey body of the sand shark washed ashore.
My grandsons, all eyes and legs and ready hands
pressed in to find out more about this small castaway
of waves.
With water-filled bucket and ready hearts
they were going to save this baby shark,
from the killing land and choking air.
They approached the creature
with its red gills flared, and with care,
with greatest care, hoisted its flailing body up,
slipped it into the bucket's plastic mouth,
filled with salt water from the sea,
the shark's tail wagging like the need
to be free,
as the oldest one waded out into the sea,
searching for the best wave to carry the shark home,
back to the depths where it might roam
the open waters,
far from the riptides and the threat of scalding sands,
far from the curious eyes and cruel hands of young boys
who might not understand that life is sacred
and deserves a second chance.

Some Mothers

Some mothers eat their children,
salt their little lives with hungry tears
to tenderize those tiny vittles.
These are the mothers who use
expensive spice and sherries rare,
each a device to make a gustatory delight,
so much to prepare
for the day, the hour, the moment
they feel right to light the stove,
turn the heat up to high, then repose.
These are the mothers who never miss a beat
to be the first in line,
knives sharpened, forks with polished tines,
ready to eat.
These are the mothers who are more than willing
to do anything—even spilling a little blood,
to dine on their children's roasted flesh.
These are the mothers who after the last of the meat
with a splinter of child bone, will pick, then suck their teeth,
satiated and so replete at the end of the day
glowing with the knowing that they
have had their own way.

Continuum

When love dies, or is stolen,
or driven away, then there is
a void in space, in time,
and the race begins to fill the gap in,
to make whole again, the sublime
pattern of cosmic branes.
Disbelief comes first,
followed by pain,
then fear, then the curse of
vengeance that slowly creates
a room for resentment
to give birth to hate,
for all that was to give,
for all that was to take,
until the scar is finally formed
and makes its presence known.
One more bump in the ongoing road
to healing,
one more chance to find the feeling
that life is worth it, after all.

Time for Two

If time is different for each of us
unless we are next to each other,
then loneliness becomes a toss
between genetic exile and individual choice.
If this be the case, I say rejoice.
Let's eyes to eyes, lips to lips, breasts to breasts
lie down upon the ground, press our naked best
together till all our twos become ones
in the heat of the everlasting sun,
till we slow time's endless flow.

Cashing In

Because a family is a construct
and a construct, like a china plate
or a crystal vase, can be shattered,
I've stopped thinking of family
as anything more than it is,
a beautiful but fragile object that
can be bought, bequeathed, broken, or stolen,
accidentally lost, deliberately sold,
or with little thought, simply thrown away.
So many thrift shops and garage sales to sell
the bits and pieces of our marked-down lives
for pennies on the dollar.
Though we may attempt a protest, maybe,
even an occasional holler,
in the end, in the very end, we meet the going price—
a heart for a nickel, a soul for a dime,
cashing in our lives for small change.

The Master Baiter

When I was young, I could bait a hook
better than anyone in my family could.
It was an art, really.
Digging the blood worms the night before,
lifting them undulating, a living gore,
the clods of mud, raised in the air.
I was Perseus holding Medusa's hair,
pressing it carefully with my hand,
into the Maxwell House coffee can,
till it was full of living ground.
When the next day finally came around,
we'd rise before dawn, river bound.
Each eager fisherman, staked his spot.
then came the moment that I got
to show my skill as the worm and I went will to will.
The silver barb between forefinger and thumb,
the worm squirming at what was to come.
One quick push was all it took
to slip the crawler onto the hook,
with enough of its tail left on the end
to dance in the water, to tease and to tempt
the sunnies and bass passing by,
a delectable repast to the gold foil eye
of some hungry fish.
All that was left was to cast and to sit.
Then wiping the slime from my fingers and thumb,
I watched the striped bobber shine in the sun.
I strained for signs of the first little twists
That would prove that I knew how to bait for a fish.

The Apprentice

On the beach
in the wind
he stands
with blue plastic
spade in his hands,
twirling round,
draws a circle
in the sand,
small necromancer
taking first whiff
of the grand
celebration of nature.
The wild gusts
tussle his hair
the white caps thrust
their spray in the air,
and the child trusts
that life will be fair
as long as he is loved.

When They Come Back

When they come back to the condo,
it's like coming home,
a place that's safe,
no division of property here,
no his, no hers,
no pets packed off to the SPCA.
At the condo, it's always the same:
Grandma and Grandpa,
movies and games,
goodnights and God blesses,
and everyone stays the night.
And in the morning
after breakfast, right
to the beach to boogie board on the waves
and to dig in the sand,
to watch the gulls fly and to plan
a castle with a moat wide enough
to save it from the rush of waves.

The Pretenders

Divorce can be an easy thing.
Divide the assets; take off the ring.
Find another for a fling,
once the papers have been filed.
His time and her time
with the children
alimony and child support
in fulfillment
are all it takes to make amends.
Thus the rituals of love's end.
And not to worry,
there are family and friends
to ease a conscience, to tie up loose ends.
Just try not to notice how the children pretend
when asked if they are happy.

Songs of Nature

River Tricks

The river moves, a slow rhythm of waves and loops
next to, through him,
the eddies and currents of his life flowing,
the worlds outside and within, growing
in the wisdom of this earth but not the grace.
He's a travelling man who has lost his place in transition,
a broken-winged loon coming in to crash land,
a magician who has run out of tricks and with no plan
to get the woman out of the box, to pull out streams of
colorful silk scarves, to make paper flowers out of thin air,
to tap of his wand and make white doves appear.
It's the end of the road; it's the song of the swan,
and still the river runs, on and on,
its melody deep; its silence strong.

Of Mice and Friends

I saved a baby mouse today, a child of the fields,
battleship grey with ebony eyes and soft white ears,
about the size of my thumb, raised on its rears,
with forearms that hung between wonder and despair,
as it scurried back and forth, stranded on the stair with
nowhere to go.
The wedge of corrugated board I found made a nice bridge
for the mouse who after a few rounds of back and forth
climbed aboard without a sound and clung spread eagle facing
    down
as I gently raised him up.
Tiny wayfarer, he was just a pup, a bit of grey fluff, riding the tip
of the board, rigidly clinging with tiny claws as I moved down
    the hall
and through the glass doors, out into a field, near an oak tree
where I lowered the board into tall weeds.
The little mouse leapt down and scampered off with ease,
its small body designed to loop and to squeeze through
the tangle and root.
I watched the earth swallow this tiny truth,
link between the worlds of mice and men.
Life is precious and quite easy to lose
and survival, a miracle, that requires
a friend, with a determined will and the heart to choose.

Summer Love

July arrives, hot vengeance,
all body glove and glistening
as the wax-fleshed maple leaves
in swan-shaped ecstasies,
neck-stemmed elegance, glory in green.
How they shimmer and please the hungry eye,
turning up the heat on sultry July morns
whose cool shadows curl in corners and lie,
black dogs wagging dark tails
of relief from the heat that licks
a salt-tongued melting that runs
off the body, but sticks to the heart,
concupiscence is a careful art.
July is hot comings and goings, out of control,
Dog Days stoking the fire in the soul,
fanning the heat till the mind explodes
a thousand fantasies that break all the rules,
all the molds, a frenzied, driven dancing,
both kind and cruel,
the stuff summer loves are made of.

Summer's Colors

Summer is back, sultry mistress
with her greenleaf glistening ways,
luring me into shadows where my
imagination plays, turning tricks,
sweet seductions on display,
lutes and wine, weeping willow veils
entwine, in memory of Salome
keeping perfect time with each
sensuous beat.
I seek. I find.
The sweet center of the peach,
ritual succulence, where fleshy pit
has its seat.
With tongue and teeth I dislodge it
from its russet groove,
and gently move down to lick and eat,
each time with feeling new.
How does one measure pleasure in the
midst of the feast?
I spend myself in the leisure of
summer's hot dreams,
taking all she has to give,
all the heat beat luster of her schemes.
I lie in oiled decadence; my chest heaves
desire up and out,
each glorious wave a masterpiece of being,
a reason to shout,
about learning to obey the body's call
of touching
of tasting
of seeing all
of summer's colors.

The Light

Today I was one with the light,
prancing on the leaves
of the tulip tree,
bright scoops of me,
all Chinese fan dance
and flickering chance,
shadow and sunshine
romancing the breeze
with staccato winks
and shimmering tease.
I caught a glimpse of the divine
spinning glowing threads
mending the tattered hem
of destiny,
Basting the edges of
the living and the dead,
till all was one glowing whole,
a single piece,
where I might find my place
and shine.

Serenity

Out here, in the limitless blue
of sea and sky and me, a trinity
I've always longed for, always knew
was meant to be,
no beginning,
no end,
just an ongoing expanse,
a dance that pretends
infinity.
If I did not know better,
I would see God all around me,
an indigo dream of forever being,
is, was, has been, will be,
ever and a day, endlessly
rolling, wave after silken wave.
There is no need for more than this
serenity, of time, of matter, and of space.

I Shall Sing of Beauties

I have learned to cultivate a deep love
for the abundant beauties of this world,
countless small wonders of everyday sight,
from the iris's purple petals to the firefly's golden light.
I've learned to marvel at the sunburst
in the dandelion's velvet face,
to meditate on the Kelly green
of the soft-furred moss that grows between
the rocks in the cool, deep shade.
I have mastered the art of listening
to the brook's burbling song,
and have happily placed my ready cheek in
the west wind's soothing palm.
I have studied the dance of shifting clouds
in their waltz across the sky.
I have rolled with the thunder of the surf
and with the shifting sands have sighed.
I have wept for joy at the rose's birth
and wept for sorrow when it died.
I have greeted the dawn with open heart
and the night with naked soul.
I have counted the glistening starry tears
and the years that have made me old.
But I am rescued by the robin's song
and rise on the barn swallow's wings.
And as long as I have breath and voice,
this world's beauties will I sing.

Mycocepurus-Smithii

There is a species of ants—all females—
who reproduce by cloning their queen.
No male pretenders to the throne
of these able, mandibled Amazons
who have given up the battle of the sexes,
left Mars and Venus neatly confined in the net,
the way modern man captures the beetles of Japan
in pheromoned bags of pleasured death.
This warrior race has set down bow and arrow,
biochemical plague, and atomic bomb,
has taken the evil out of knowledge,
has learned to reproduce, to rule without harm,
has chosen to remain with Gaia in order to farm
the floral fungi that each might eat her fill,
live long enough to grow wise in the ways
of serving a greater will.

Dragonfly

I have seen mystery in the mica mesh of a dragonfly's wings,
vibrating light, divine shimmerings of flight,
neon blue body, thin as a pin, dancing in air,
walking on water, rich and rare,
a beauty that borders beyond compare,
a thing of styled elegance, glittering with grace.
I have watched it hover, watched it rise and race
above the salty marsh,
a living jewel that dives and darts,
pure illumination that piques imagination,
elicits from the heart, a standing ovation,
inspires artists to Tiffany creations,
dragon of beauty, of truth, of dreams.

Summer Passion

I can feel it in the air,
the sultry green of summer
stepping lightly in the breeze,
shedding her fox club green
among late May's falling petals
and trembling leaves,
the branches stirring to receive
cool undulations for the steamy dreams
of July and August, yet to come.
It is a moment beautiful and rare, one
that lifts me with white witch arms,
lets me see the coming charms
of summer's warm delights,
feel earth's pulse, the sweat of grass
on hot and humid nights.
It is a vision that lasts mere seconds
and then quite suddenly takes flight,
like the butterfly or the bumblebee
who set upon a bloom to feed
till drawn away by scent or sight
to proceed most quickly to the next,
exercising an eternal rite, doing their best
to sanctify the passion of this world.

Road Stop

A starling landed on the front bumper
of a big rig heading west,
for a moment, flicked its tail, side to side,
and with inquisitive glance, cocked its head.
Then, like a hungry patron satisfied
with the road stop it had so timely espied,
took a leap and went inside
to eat its fill at the grill buffet.
I watched it flutter up and down
at all the repast to be found:
mosquito, wasp, and butterfly,
ladybug, grasshopper, and tatter-winged moth
wind mashed and perfectly radiator fried,
crispy entrees at the perfect cost
for any bright-eyed wayfarer in between flights.
I watched the starling pick and choose,
eat its fill, and then, when through,
upon the bumper, stop to preen,
arrange its feathers, straight and clean,
then with a gesture, much like a prayer,
spread its wings and take to air.

The Misplaced

I saw a hermit crab struggling with a shell
too big for his little legs to carry, his small claws to drag.
I watched him disappear in the calcium mouth,
rock it steadily till it overturned,
then in rumble, bumble motion,
make a creeping thing of its new home.
The scuttling squatter born to dwell
in mechanical rhythm began to roam,
looking for a safer place to hide,
taking the sun, the gulls, the waves, the feet,
the shoveling hands of children in stride.
Then I thought, how often my own life
has been lost and found, and the wrong size,
sometimes too small for my dreams, my desires,
sometimes too large.
I thought of times I longed to cover myself
and from the burdens of my own life hide,
to crawl away to safer sands,
ignore the feet that would gladly crush,
the many ruthless, grabbing hands,
a place of respite, where I might reside.

Cloud Dragon

Once, when he was very young,
he dreamed he could ride a dragon made of clouds,
soar the infinite blue of day,
shouting aloud for eagles and geese
to get out of his way,
his arms thrown wide,
extended from his sides,
a Merlin child who had learned to fly
by the power of wild thinking.
How he conjured beings from long ago,
beckoned spirits to come and go,
the lightning dancing off his fingertips,
the spells and wishes falling from his lips,
like clusters of shooting stars.
Thus, he spent his days in dutiful ways,
closing the wounds, healing the scars
of a world that had drifted far, too far,
from fancy.

The Fairytale

I saw a picture of a tree frog that swallowed a twinkling light.
Poor thing, how could it have known the little blinker would
 hold tight
to its electric wire,
and when it flashed, the befuddled frog glowed in the night,
like some amphibious firefly, blinking dark to bright,
like some neon bar sign, flashing delight
to all who come and open wide,
like the little frog who had inside him
the difference between night and day,
who couldn't disgorge it and hop away,
a little frog prince, forever changed,
the need to eat deranged as the need to breed.
The fruit of his desires, glowing within,
like the sudden knowledge of good and evil,
perfect symbol of original sin,
darkness, then light, then darkness again.
It was a strange picture, and I knew the minute I saw it
that the fairy tale had a bad ending.

The Spring Inside

Watching the earth grow green,
someone inside me dreams
of being young again,
of looking for fairies asleep in the flowers,
of finding elves holding court in the bowers,
of discovering gnomes mining for gold in the caves,
something in the green slowly wakes
the sleeping child deep inside,
and for a while, a very short while,
I am young again, with a tender heart and a willing smile,
and the belief that this world is good.

Beauty Views

Some look for beauty beyond the sky,
seeing its essence in a golden eye.
Others find fairness in a pale moon.
Some seek glamour in a tune.
Some hold beauty in a rare cut gem.
Some call exquisite the words from the pen.
Some call stunning, a statue carved.
Some find perfection in a perfumed jar.
There are those who see beauty in youth's smooth face.
There are those who find beauty in the body's grace.
To all who are drawn to beauty's power,
I offer the bloom of a single flower.

Time to Go

I've been looking through the raindrops too long.
Time to turn on the wipers, change the tune on the radio,
find a new song for the road.
Time to set the GPS for the sun,
Time to rev the engine for the run
that will give me pleasure, make me smile,
allow me some stops for unplanned leisure,
give me the chance to take a while to live this world,
learn to treasure flowers,
learn to listen to trees,
learn to sing with the birds,
learn to dance in the breeze.
Yes, I've been too long in the rain,
looking out through the tear-stained pane.
Time to get going, time to set myself free,
time that I regain the joy of being me.

The Coital

They come; they go, talking about love
as if they know the real meaning,
as if the cock, the cunt,
were the only players in the game.
So little time for the heart, the mind.
Always the same, a story of who comes first ,
comes best, comes longest, the rest
left unattended like bridges and fences
that go unmended,
until boundaries are blurred,
until collapse occurs.
Then everyone shakes their heads in sorrow
for the ones who drown.
Then there is talk of tomorrow,
of what has been lost,
of what has been found,
beyond night's secrets, between the sheets of the bed.
Then we reach for something to believe in,
someone to conceive in,
something to pretend there is meaning.

First Blood

A morning in early May after a night of steady rain,
a puddle glistens under blue sky.
Two cock robins, breast to breast, beak to beak, vie
for the privilege to bathe.
A sudden dart, then head against head
they tumble around the ground.
Tails flare and beaks embed,
the silence, shattered, by animal sound.
Down and feathers are left behind
as the rancorous pair twist and grind
along the puddle's edge.
The water, a holy innocence, reflects the daybreak brawl,
with room enough for two to bathe.
Instead, the warriors thrash and maul
a battering of battle wings, till one beak sinks
deep in the flesh of the other's neck, and the flood begins
to well up in red velvet tenderness, the very first blood of
spring.

A Storm by Any Other Name

At first, I thought it was snow,
a flurry of white flakes in the night.
Flicking the high beams showed
a shower of apple blossoms
that twirled and glowed,
dancing in the bright streams of light.
They rushed against the windshield,
In sheer delight, I opened the windows
to watch the wayfaring petals blow.
Some pirouetted across the dash.
Some delicately landed in my lap.
Others, like velvet lips, softly kissed my face.
It was a sanctifying moment;
I was experiencing grace
bestowed by the bounty of trees.
I felt the tug of eternity as I was most auspiciously
bathed in the beauty of petal truth.

The Landscape

I take the sable brush tip of my soul,
dip it into the bright hues of being,
bring forth a van Gogh sun,
then, again, a swatch of Prussian blue,
swirling around in wavering lines.
Next come the hills of bright chartreuse,
billowing blades of grass in wind,
followed by bright orange poppies,
whose petals dance on the tips of their stems.
Finally, an apple green cottage,
thatched with a lavender roof,
trimmed with white window boxes
filled with flowers of beauty and truth.

Body Song

The body has its own song,
knowing when to hum quietly to itself,
when to burst full-throated into duet,
when to fall like leaves, October gold.
The body syncopates its beats
in quick arrivals, in slow retreats,
a full note held till the moment is reached.
The body is expert in refrain,
knowing when to give, when to receive,
again, and again, and again.
The body knows how to leave its audience,
shouting in acclaim,
demanding with roses,
ENCORE, by any other name.

I Watched a Monarch

I watched a monarch take to flight,
wings as bright as Japanese fans,
rice paper flutterings in the air,
above the flowers till he chose to land
long enough to probe and sip
with proboscis sleek and delicate,
the tender throats of the garden's fair
until an unexpected wind
swept away this winged king.
I watched him swirl in velvet ascent.
Here, then there, he came and went,
spiraling high into the blue.
I watched the dance of his orange hue,
until it finally disappeared,
this king of spring so rich and rare,
whose regal splendor, beyond compare,
in beauty, ruled the day.

P.C. Scheponik is an associate professor of English at Montgomery County Community College. His poetry has appeared in *One Trick Pony*, *The Thirteenth Warrior Review*, Blue *Ink Press*, *Asterius Press*, and *Black Bear Review*. His first published book of poetry was *Psalms to Padre Pio*, a collection of poems celebrating the beatification of famed stigmatist St. Pio of Pietrelcina. His most recent publication, *And the Sun Still Dared to Shine*, is a collection of poems remembering the Holocaust, published by Mazo Publishing in 2011. P.C. Scheponik lives with his wife, Shirley. Together they escape as often as they can to their seaside getaway.

www.ingramcontent.com/pod-product-compliance
Ingram Content Group UK Ltd.
Pitfield, Milton Keynes, MK11 3LW, UK
UKHW020237250726
13967UKWH00001B/422

9 781257 058822